FACT CAT

THE WRIGHT BROTHERS

First Flight

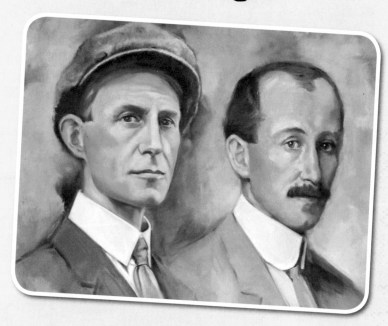

Jane Bingham

FACT Cat

Get your paws on this fantastic new mega-series from Wayland!

Join our Fact Cat on a journey of fun learning about every subject under the sun!

Published in paperback in 2017 by Wayland
© Hodder and Stoughton Limited 2017

Wayland is an imprint of Hachette Children's Group
Part of Hodder & Stoughton
Carmelite House
50 Victoria Embankment
London EC4Y 0DZ

Produced for Wayland by
White-Thomson Publishing Ltd
www.wtpub.co.uk
+44 (0) 843 208 7460

Editor: Jane Bingham
Design: Rocket Design (East Anglia) Ltd
Fact Cat illustrations: Shutterstock/Julien Troneur
Other illustrations: Stefan Chabluk
Consultant: Kate Ruttle

A catalogue for this title is available from the British Library

ISBN: 978 0 7502 9039 5
Library eBook ISBN: 978 0 7502 9038 8

Dewey Number: 629.1'3'0922-dc23
10 9 8 7 6 5 4 3 2 1

Wayland is a division of Hachette Children's Group,
an Hachette UK company.
www.hachette.co.uk

Printed and bound in China

Picture and illustration credits:
Cover (foreground) Library of Congress/Science Faction/Science and Society/Superstock (background) Science and Society/Superstock; p.1 Dreamstime/Wangkun Jia; p.4 Wikimedia; p.5 Dreamstime/Wangkun Jia; p.6 (left) Library of Congress; p.6 (right) Wikimedia; p.7 Stefan Chabluk; p.8 Wikimedia; p.9 Dreamstime/Kajornyot; p.10 Stefan Chabluk; p.11 Wikimedia; p.12 Wikimedia; p.13 Wikimedia; p.14 Stefan Chabluk; p.15 Dreamstime/Dean Neitman; p.16 Wikimedia; p.17 Science and Society/Superstock; p.18 Corbis Fine Art; p.19 Science and Society/Superstock; p.20 Library of Congress/Superstock; p.21 Wikimedia.

The author, Jane Bingham, is a writer and editor specialising in children's educational publishing.

The consultant, Kate Ruttle, is a literacy expert and SENCO, and teaches in Suffolk.

FACT CAT FACT

There is a question for you to answer on each spread in this book. You can check your answers on page 24.

CONTENTS

A WONDERFUL DREAM

People have always dreamed of being able to fly. But it took a very long time for this dream to come true. The first **successful** flight was made in a hot air balloon.

The Montgolfier brothers made the first balloon flight in 1843. Which country did they come from?

Wilbur

Orville

In the 1890s, some **inventors** built **gliders**. The first gliders didn't stay up in the air for long. Then, in 1902, brothers Wilbur and Orville Wright built a glider that could fly. After that, they designed a plane.

Orville Wright made the world's first plane flight in December 1903.

FACT CAT FACT

The first balloon flight took place 60 years before the first plane flight.

5

GROWING UP

Wilbur and Orville came from a large family. There were seven Wright children, but two of them died when they were very young.

Wilbur

Orville

Wilbur was born in 1867 in the state of Indiana, USA. Orville was born in 1871 in the state of Ohio. Can you find Indiana and Ohio on a map of the USA?

While they were still at school, the brothers set up a **printing press**. They used the press to print newspapers.

The brothers made **kites** which they flew. They also made a toy **helicopter**. It had a twisted elastic band to help it fly.

toy helicopter

twisted elastic band

box kite

FACT CAT FACT

Wilbur invented a machine that folded newspapers. It folded the papers the brothers had printed so they could be sent through the post.

BICYCLES AND GLIDERS

In 1892 the Wright brothers opened a bicycle repair shop. Soon they were designing bicycles to sell. They also became interested in gliders. **Several** people were designing gliders in the 1890s.

Otto Lilienthal

Otto Lilienthal was a German inventor who built his own glider. He made several flights before he crashed and died. In which year did he die?

The brothers made plans to build their own glider. They studied birds to see how they **steered** through the air.

Birds twist their wing-tips to help them turn. The Wright brothers decided to copy this move.

FACT CAT FACT

Wilbur and Orville had a friend who wanted them to build cars. But the brothers weren't interested in cars.

A NEW KIND OF GLIDER

First, the brothers built a very large box kite. They used this kite to test out their ideas for a glider.

When the kite strings were pulled, the wing-tips twisted and the kite turned. The **elevator** helped to lift the kite up through the air.

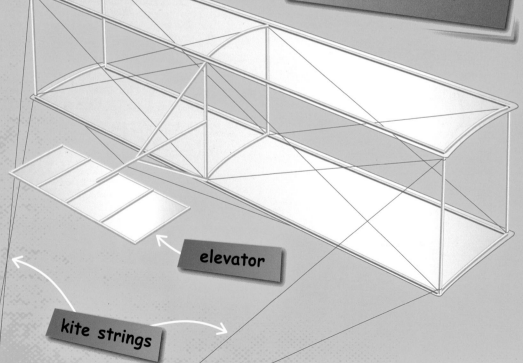

elevator

kite strings

At last, the brothers were happy with their kite.
Then they built a glider that was steered by a **pilot**.
They tested the glider many times, but it always crashed!

The brothers tested their glider in a very windy place called Kitty Hawk. Which American state is Kitty Hawk in?

FACT CAT FACT

The pilot steered the glider by pulling on cords that were fixed to each wing-tip. He could also raise and lower the elevator.

MAKING CHANGES

Even though their glider was not a success, the brothers did not give up. Instead, they decided to change its design. They used a **wind tunnel** to test out their ideas.

This model shows Orville with his wind tunnel. He looked through a window on the top of the tunnel.

The brothers' new glider had long, narrow wings that were curved on top. It moved smoothly through the air.

The new glider stayed up in the air! It could fly for more than 182 metres (600 feet). How does that **distance** compare with the length of a football pitch?

FACT CAT FACT

Both the Wright brothers were **expert** pilots. They took turns at flying their glider.

GETTING IT RIGHT

The brothers kept making changes to their glider. They added a **rudder** so it could move from side to side.

The elevator moved the glider up and down. The rudder moved it from side to side. The wing-tips could be twisted to make the glider turn.

rudder

cord attached to wing-tip

elevator

FACT CAT FACT

The early gliders and planes were all **biplanes**, with two sets of wings.

The new glider could be steered in all directions. Now it needed an engine to turn it into an aeroplane. In November 1902 the brothers started work on their first plane.

The brothers designed their plane in their bicycle repair shop. What was the name of the town where their cycle shop was?

THE WRIGHT CYCLE CO.

FIRST FLIGHT

Wilbur and Orville couldn't find anyone to make the engine. So they built their own. The engine was linked to two wooden **propellers**.

This model shows how the plane worked. The propellers spun around and drove the plane through the air.

propellers

engine

On December 17 1903 the *Wright Flyer* was ready to be tested. Orville was the pilot. Wilbur ran beside the plane until it took off. It was the first successful aeroplane flight!

The *Wright Flyer* stayed in the air for about 12 seconds. Can you find out what distance it covered?

wooden track

FACT CAT FACT

The brothers built a wooden track for their plane to run along. The plane ran very fast along the track before it took off.

FLYING TAKES OFF

In 1904, Wilbur and Orville built *Flyer II*, but it had problems taking off. Then they designed *Flyer III*. It had a seat for the pilot.

Flyer III was a very successful aircraft. In 1905, it flew for 39 kilometres (24 miles).

FACT CAT FACT

The brothers built a large wooden **catapult** to help **launch** *Flyer II* into the air.

In 1909, the brothers set up the Wright Company to make and sell aeroplanes. They also trained pilots to fly their planes.

The next step was to add a **passenger** seat. Female passengers tied their skirts round their ankles with rope. Why do you think they did this?

LAST YEARS

In 1912, Wilbur caught **typhoid** and died. He was only 45 years old. After his brother's death, Orville stopped flying. He sold his share of the Wright Company.

This photograph shows Orville when he was in his fifties. He died in 1948 at the age of 76.

FACT CAT FACT

Orville made a toy for his nephews and nieces. It was called Flips and Flops and it was a model **acrobat** who performed **somersaults**.

The Wright brothers' **invention** changed the world forever. Thanks to Wilbur and Orville, we can fly around the world in passenger planes. **Astronauts** have even flown to the Moon!

This photograph shows the launch of the *Apollo 11* spacecraft. Can you find out which year *Apollo 11* landed on the Moon?

QUIZ

Try to answer the questions below. Look back through the book to help you. Check your answers on page 24.

1 The Wright brothers were the first people to fly in a hot air balloon. True or not true?

a) true

b) not true

2 In which direction did the rudder move the *Wright Flyer*?

a) from side to side

b) up and down

c) forwards and backwards

3 How many propellers did the *Wright Flyer* have?

a) one

b) four

c) two

4 The Wright brothers used a large catapult to help launch *Flyer II* into the air. True or not true?

a) true

b) not true

5 How old was Wilbur Wright when he died?

a) 29

b) 45

c) 76

GLOSSARY

acrobat someone who performs very difficult jumps, rolls and other moves

astronaut someone who travels in space

biplane a plane or a glider with two sets of wings

catapult a large machine used for sending objects into the air

distance the amount of space between two places

elevator the part of a plane that is used to raise or lower it in the air

expert very good at doing something

glider a very light aircraft without an engine that flies by floating on air currents

helicopter an aircraft with rotating blades on top

invention a new machine or idea

inventor someone who creates a new machine or idea

kite a frame covered in material, plastic or paper that is attached to a string or strings and flown in the wind

launch to send an object into the air

passenger someone who travels in a vehicle, such as a plane, train or car

pilot someone who flies an aircraft

printing press a machine that uses ink to produce words and pictures on a page

propeller a set of blades that turn very fast to push a plane through the air

rudder a flap attached to a plane or boat that is used for steering

several a small number of people or things

somersault a roll that is performed by tucking the head into the chest and rolling forward

steer to make something go in the right direction

successful doing what was planned or wanted

typhoid a very serious disease that is usually caught from dirty water

wind tunnel a machine to test how objects move through air

INDEX

ANSWERS

Pages 4–21

page 4: The Montgolfier brothers came from France.

page 8: Otto Lilienthal died in 1896.

page 11: Kitty Hawk is in North Carolina.

page 13: A football pitch measures about 100 metres (328 ft). The Wright glider flew for almost the length of two football pitches.

page 15: The Wright brothers' cycle shop was in Dayton, Ohio.

page 17: The first flight of the *Wright Flyer* covered a distance of about 37 metres (121 feet).

page 19: Female passengers tied their skirts round their ankles to stop the skirts flying up in the wind!.

page 21: *Apollo 11* landed on the Moon in 1969.

Quiz answers

1   b) not true. The Montgolfier brothers made the first hot air balloon flight.

2   a) The rudder moved the *Wright Flyer* from side to side.

3   c) The *Wright Flyer* had two propellers.

4   a) true

5   b) Wilbur Wright died aged 45.